Love Is Love but... Business Is Business

Love Is Love but... Business Is Business

MERLE H. HORWITZ
Attorney-at-law

QUILL

New York 1983

Published in association with Stan Corwin Productions.

Library of Congress Cataloging in Publication Data

Horwitz, Merle H.
Love is love but— business is business.

1. Unmarried couples—Legal status, laws, etc.—
United States. I. Title.
KF538.H67 1983 346.7301′6 83-2878
ISBN 0-688-02062-3 (pbk.) 347.30616

Printed in the United States of America

First Quill Edition

1 2 3 4 5 6 7 8 9 10

BOOK DESIGN BY BERNARD SCHLEIFER

Contents

Love Is Love but... Business Is Business

I. Introduction

YOU'RE IN LOVE.

Great!

When was the last time? How often have you been in this state of bliss?

Or are you just very alone, after a divorce, after a death?

No one can think straight in this condition. Convincing yourself that aloneness is the equivalent of forced solitary confinement can make you do things you'll regret.

If you want to get married don't be deterred. Marriage is marvelous. But how about a trial period? Coming back to reality may be painful but not as painful as divorce.

People live together nowadays. They *cohabit.*

Men and women of all ages enter into this state of being. They don't marry. Today parents ask their children not to marry—not yet. Youngsters ask their widowed or divorced parents not to marry. They say, try it first; they don't want to see a new husband or wife take advantage of the lifetime accumulations of their mom or dad.

People don't want to carry on sleazy two-apartment affairs, wear phony wedding rings on weekend vacations, or worry themselves to death about what the social circle thinks. Good sense is beginning to triumph.

However, new court decisions and the probability of even more widespread legal decisions throughout the fifty states have caused all these couples new concern. Just living together can create property rights for each. You can't live together for extended periods of time in a marital kind of existence without expecting some kind of marital-type rights to arise.

Women cannot be expected to shrug their shoulders and walk away when love has flown.

Men cannot be expected to sacrifice to a liberated woman's career and shrug and walk away when love has flown.

So, if you think that LOVE IS LOVE even when you don't get married, think again. We keep telling you—BUSINESS IS BUSINESS—*especially when you're in love.*

Some unique problems can arise in these cohabiting situations, such as when you're married to one person and living part time with another. You know, captain's paradise. Or, when you are in the process of a divorce and are living with someone else at the same time, and this someone else conspires with you to hide assets from your spouse. Suppose the assets are put in your roommate's name. Then suppose you marry your roommate? Who is entitled to what?

Or suppose you want to buy a house, and you use your own money and put it in your name, but your roommate makes occasional mortgage payments toward the house or helps you fix it up, landscape it, decorate it or in any way make it more valuable. Then what? In whose name will the phone be? Whose number? Gas? Electricity?

A variety of rights arise in all of these situations. Worse than the rights which may arise are the *claims* and the corresponding legal hassles which will undoubtedly arise if you do not have a contract.

When you cohabit as *your* way of life and have children, things can become very difficult. It's one of the situations covered in the question-and-answer section.

Usually you can approach the business aspect of your love relationship more easily in a cohabiting situation than in an expected marital situation. Each of you generally agrees that you are going to live together and will see how it goes. The absolute blind commitment of twenty-year-old newlyweds is not quite there. Accordingly, you should approach the property question directly and bluntly. The issues will arise in the natural course of your discussions anyway.

You can trust your live-in partner without trusting either your own memory or your partner's memory. I have a good memory but not an infallible one.

As soon as you begin discussing money wiith your proposed new roommate you will see his or her true colors.

You will see that a contract is vital to avoid unnecessary fear and possible later misery. This does not mean that you are programming an eventual failure of the relationship, just the opposite. Settling the financial areas of your life reduces tension, suspicion and worry. Every business reduces its vital affairs to the written word. What is more vital than love?

II. What's in This Book?

THIS BOOK CONTAINS an actual contract which you may fill out, choosing between optional paragraphs to suit your situation. It is valid in all of the United States. It relies on contract principles of basic American-English jurisprudence. Even if you think you disagree with some of the paragraphs, use them. They have been developed after extensive study of the law, many court cases and reflection. For instance, the contract provides for the sale of jointly owned assets acquired during the relationship upon the termination of the relationship. There is no way to handle this situation, except to sell the assets or to agree to keep them intact (which is provided). All other alternatives ask for trouble. The contract also provides for legal arbitration to settle disputes. Arbitration is cheaper and faster than the customary judicial systems but it also permits *legal enforcement* of the terms of the agreement.

All real property assets should be acquired as *Tenants in Common*. Use these words on deeds and other *real* property documents. They are the essential words necessary to carry out the acquisition.

When you acquire personal property, such as furniture and the like, have a clear understanding as to its ownership. If it belongs to both, don't complain when you are held accountable to this fact.

Your complaints are an expression of anger resulting from a mini-divorce and not an expression of ownership.

This book also contains an extensive question-and-answer section which sets out to answer each of your questions. However, the contract itself answers nearly everything and tells you what you should agree upon. You can change the terms of the contract if you wish, but be careful the way you use new clauses or different agreements. Where there is a choice within the contract, cross out what does not apply to you and initial it. Make things *very* clear.

The contract contains a clause permitting a review and a change in ownership of assets separately or jointly acquired. It does *not require* a change. It's a good idea to review because it gives you a chance to think about where you are heading. You can write out all changes, sign and date and attach the additional sheet to the contract with a staple.

The hardest idea to deal with is when one of the partners has children. Some funds will, of necessity, be used directly or indirectly for the children—it can't be helped. The party without the child will have to accept this situation or find another situation.

The question-and-answer section deals with the questions of needing a lawyer, a notary, witnesses, and how to enforce the agreement efficiently and inexpensively. Also, the interesting question of a *successful* cohabitation is answered in the Special Problems section. Are marriage and a prenuptial or marital agreement far away?

III. Special Problems

EVERY RELATIONSHIP HAS its own problems. Mother-daughter, father-son, partner-junior partner, master-mistress.

Cohabitation has its own peculiar problems.

What do you put on the mailbox? Who gets the phone number? Who gets the season tickets? Who subscribes to the newspaper and Book-of-the-Month Club? Marriage is easy. You fight about everything until little parts of the puzzle are resolved. But cohabitation is one of those relationships that doesn't go well with major resolutions of great psychological importance to the partners. It certainly does not go well with bickering. Somehow a married couple has a special license to bicker. That's partly why you prefer cohabitation first with a good contract over a marriage. Just remember, no one has guaranteed you a smooth, untroubled existence. If that's what you want—get thee to a nunnery or take vows in a Tibetan monastery.

These are the special problems:

1. *Leases*

In whose name will the lease on the house or apartment be taken? Both or one?

First of all, let's get rid of your notion that you can move into *her* house or apartment or that you can move into *his* house or apartment. *It can't be done!*

Territorial imperatives are facts of life. His apartment is *his* and her apartment is *hers*. One party will always be an outsider. The trinkets and the decor and the plants and the ashtrays and the chair in the corner and the lamp over the couch will forever get in the other person's way. Where you put the towels and how many glasses go into the bar and into the kitchen will be the province of the one who already resides at the location.

Don't be foolish enough to think that *you* can maturely handle all this apparent nonsense. You can't. Recognize it as an important part of each person's life. Respect it and go find neutral territory.

Although it's preferable not to take a long-term lease, nowadays a good price on the apartment or house for more than one year is too compelling to pass up. Take the lease in *both* names giving each a possessory sense about his or her home. Put first and last months' rent down *and*, if possible, deposit one additional month's rent into a joint savings account. In the event of termination of the relationship the one remaining need not worry:

a. If you have a short-term lease you can move very quickly.
b. New roommates sharing a good apartment at a decent price are much easier to come by than you think.
c. Your landlord will be pleased if you move out. He won't sue you, just re-rent the place at a higher rent. In some cases he will pay you to move depending on the rent he can *then* expect to get.
d. The additional deposit of rent can be used to cover an extra month, or shared by each for moving expenses. You have plenty of time to plan ahead.

In any event you cannot *eliminate all* the risks involved in cohabitation. Some risks will remain, and this is appropriate. A contract is provided which clarifies all major financial and property concerns.

2. *Real Property*

The two of you may want to purchase a home or invest in real estate together in varying proportions. This is easy. Take a deed in each pro-rata share as "Tenants in Common." The deed would read: "John Doe, an undivided 50 percent interest as a Tenant in Common and Jane Roe, an undivided 50 percent interest as a Tenant in Common." Each now owns half of the whole but not a specific half. You can't physically divide most parcels of real property.

The problems arise when the parties split and one wants to sell and one doesn't, or both want to keep the property.

The contract takes care of this situation. You *must* sell. You must sell to your partner or to an independent third person. If you sell to your partner you save brokerage commissions. But you will have to give reasonable terms, i.e., 30 percent down, balance due in monthly amortized payments over three years at a fair interest rate. This ties you to one another for a while. There is no perfect solution, therefore it is wisest to sell and split the proceeds. One party can't *make* the other a slave of his or her desire to hold the asset, especially when the asset can be sold for a fair market price at that time. Sell and get out and go about your life, and give up the subtle blackmail of holding on when it's all over. The "holding on" is what happens in marriage that makes the breakups so bitter.

3. *Furniture–Auto–Jewelry*

Identify each personal asset as described in the contract. Try to acquire new pieces of art or furniture separately. If John buys a coffee table, Jane should buy an equivalent piece or understand that the coffee table is John's table forevermore, until otherwise agreed in writing.

When you must or want to purchase *together* you are compelled to sell the piece and divide the proceeds appropriately. There is no other reasonably acceptable way except to agree *in writing* to keep it for a specified period of time.

When John buys Jane jewelry on her birthday or for any occasion, get used to the idea that 90 percent of the courts in the U.S. will find this a gift owned solely by the recipient. Accordingly, accept the notion of giving and give up the notion of giving and keeping at the same time. Of course, vice versa is also true. Some newly "liberated" women have a tendency to want to return such gifts and assert their independence and equality. Keep the diamonds. It's more of an assertion of equality than thinking you "owe" the return of the lucre. Men, if you buy expensive gifts for your roommate, no matter what she does, *you* did it and *you* asked for it.

4. Marriage

The issue of marriage will arise. It has a comforting sense of permanence. A nice sound.

Remember, marriage won't work if one is hesitant and feeling guilty about *not* getting married. It's the worst thing you can do. If it's going to be, you'll both know when. You can't nag, cajole or seduce a roommate into marriage and expect a successful one. Give it up. If you're not happy after a try at cohabitation and your partner doesn't want marriage, seriously consider a quick break, no matter how painful or difficult. That kind of pain is short-lived, but the depressive, daily effects of continual vague unhappiness for long periods is much worse and reveals in you a sense of degradation or worthlessness. Recognize it—grow beyond it and get out.

There are social pressures which force a marriage upon you. Don't try to argue people out of their position. Just accept the fact that some can't stand your freedom and independence and will let you hear about it. If marriage becomes the way each of you desires to go, remember the issues of tax consequences, social security problems and changes in the agreement. These questions arise in the question-and-answer section.

Introduce your roommate as Mr. ____ or Ms. ____. Don't mumble through the introduction. People will admire your forthrightness and courage. Guaranteed. Introduce one another as roommates instead of lovers or boy- or girlfriends. Nothing quite makes the situation as clear as the phrase "roommates" . . . especially if you are holding hands.

Many of your specific questions are answered in the question-and-answer portion of this book. Study the contract—read the questions and answers and trust the advice.

5. How to Split Up

Although you are not a statistic, and want and should have a commitment to permanence, the percentages are that after two or three years the relationship will blossom into marriage or terminate. Indeed, in either event the arrangement is over. Cohabitation arrangements are shorter-lived than marriages.

If the break comes, or *when* it creeps up on you, your life should be ready, financially. The distress will keep you from acting normally. But you will act more normally if you have money in the bank, a plan of action, a contract to guide you, an assurance that your legal rights are in order. You won't be forced into dependency or into a guilt trip because your roommate is dependent upon you. Each of you has to take your future seriously. There are alternative sections in the contract permitting an arrangement which involves contributions to joint affairs only in amounts you *can* afford.

If you can't negotiate a comfortable arrangement now with your roommate there is no way that you can reasonably expect the relationship to work at all. One negotiation is the same as another. If you back down now you are in for misery.

Accordingly, if and when you split up, live by the contract. You are not likely to successfully challenge it. In short, don't victimize yourself.

6. Season Tickets

Good tickets to pro sporting events and to the best local concert halls are precious commodities. It's impossible to divide them up unless you have four of them and they are split two and two in different but equal rows. So once again you must face reality. An auction isn't fair because one partner may have access to more money than another. You can put it in the contract if you want—you can roll the dice, draw straws or any other device of chance or, a good suggestion is that each have custody of the tickets for every *other* event. Alternate times of use. You can never know which event will turn out to be best at the beginning of the season. Fair for all.

7. Cohabitation While Married

This situation develops during the first months before a divorce is final or when a marriage is grinding to a halt. One partner commences living with boyfriend or girlfriend. The question-and-answer section discusses this special situation.

8. How to Broach the Subject

Doesn't he trust me? Doesn't she believe this is a real commitment? Why does it have to be in writing?

Opening salvos in the process of reaching a cohabitation contract are always fearful. And they customarily miss the point.

Trust is a false issue. Commitment is a false issue. The *real* issue is whether each truly loves the other *person* or the other's *estate*. It's hard to trust people who refuse to put their pens where their mouths are.

And it's also clear that no one can trust memory and the only substitute for memory is a writing.

You broach the subject by determining whose name is going to be on the lease, who is going to pay the mortgage or lease and in what proportion, who is going to pay the electric bill, phone bill, etc., and by telling one another that you are terribly frightened by impermanence but must face your fears before they will subside.

Only emotional adolescents will perversely avoid dealing with the real problems. You're a big person now. Even though it's difficult, you can talk about money and property without being carted off to the local depression farm. Also, you ought to trust the decent instincts of the other person. Clearing the air will be welcome.

Try this: "I think we ought to decide what will happen to us if we don't make it. It seems to me it's the only way to make sure we will. I don't want to worry about the future any more than I have to. I want to get over the tough parts now. I'm sure you feel the same."

You can do it.

IV: Cohabitation Agreement

Cohabitation Agreement
of
____________________ and ____________________

THIS CONTRACT is entered into the ______ day of ________ ____________________, 19__, by and between ________________ and ________________.

RECITALS

1. The undersigned parties (live together) or (intend to live together) but do not intend to marry and do not intend to have their legal relationship governed by the provisions of any state or federal domestic relations or family law statute or ruling. They shall be bound by this agreement and general contract principles.

2. The parties have together assisted one another in defining the terms of this cohabitation agreement and seek by this agreement to preserve and promote their individual privacy and identities.

3. The contract is not intended to nor does it encourage or discourage the relationship. The parties have entered into this contract solely to specify their agreement with regard to the ownership of real and personal property and to specify their relationship to all financial matters which may arise during and after the time they live together.

4. Each party has read this contract and understands all of the terms of the contract and understands that the agreements contained herein are binding in all respects. Each freely and in good faith chooses to enter into this cohabitation contract and fully intends it to be binding in every respect.

5. (*Use where applicable*) The party or parties, ______ and/or ______, have sought the advice of (friends) (an attorney) (relatives) before executing this agreement and have had the opportunity therefore to reflect upon all of the terms contained herein and agree that the terms are fair and reasonable.

ARTICLE I
PROPERTY, DEBTS AND LIVING EXPENSES

____________ and ____________ intend that the individual autonomy sought in the relationship shall be reflected in ownership of existing and future acquired property, in the characterization and control of income, and in the responsibility of each for living expenses and acquisition of necessary items of personal property which enable the relationship to appropriately exist. None of the terms herein depend upon the nature of the relationship between us.

1. *Property*

(a) The parties have made full disclosure to each other of all properties and assets presently owned by each of them and have described the income derived therefrom and from all other sources and agree that each party shall have sole management, control, and disposition of the property or assets specifically described in Schedule A, which is the separate property of ________, and Schedule B, which is the separate property of ________, both of which schedules are attached hereto, incorporated by reference and made a part of this contract. All earnings of each from any source whatsoever or earnings based on the existing separate property assets of each belong to each until and unless commingled or otherwise specified in this agreement.

1(a) (First Alternative)

There is no real or personal property at the present time which is owned jointly by the parties with the exception of those items listed as jointly owned items on Schedules A and B. Neither party desires to reveal to the other a specific list of all properties or assets owned other than as set forth in the schedules and is willing to accept the risk of possible later confusion resulting from this refusal.

1(a) (Second Alternative)

There is no real or personal property at the present time which is owned jointly by the parties except as set forth in Schedule A attached hereto and incorporated herein. Neither party desires to reveal to the other a specific list of assets or all properties and assets owned. However, each has prepared a separate list of properties and assets and has sealed the list in an envelope marked with their name thereon, which envelope is attached hereto and which shall remain sealed until and unless the parties or either one of them desire to terminate the relationship. The envelope shall be dated the day of the execution of this agreement and each schedule contained therein shall be fully dated.

2. *Earnings*

The parties agree that the wages, salary, other income, whether earnings or otherwise, or other distributions derived or received by either of the parties will be the separate property of such party and subject to the independent control and/or obligation of such party. In order to avoid the commingling of separate assets the parties shall maintain separate bank accounts, except as otherwise specified herein.

3. *Acquisitions*

All property, whether real or personal, acquired hereafter by either party during this relationship, whether by gift, inheritance, or any other means whatsoever, or derived as income generated from such property, shall belong exclusively to the party acquiring it and the other party shall acquire no rights in such asset.

4. *Joint Acquisitions*

In the event the parties acquire jointly any property, real, personal or otherwise, the ownership of said property will be determined in accordance with the respective monetary contributions of each party. No other method of pro rata ownership evaluation shall be employed.

5. *Joint Acquisitions—Alternative*

The parties may, by written agreement only, determine their respective interests in any item of property on a basis other than financial contribution, but such agreement shall not be effective unless written and signed. There shall be no oral transmutation of property from one status to another. We cannot, by conduct or oral statements, change the ownership of our respective property.

6. (Optional)

Annually, or sooner if necessary, the parties agree to amend Schedules A and B of this contract to include future acquired separate or joint property and any changes in the ownership of property presently described in said Schedules A and B.

7. *Voluntary Act*

Each party acknowledges that he or she has read all of the exhibits mentioned above and that each is entering into this agreement freely, voluntarily, and with full knowledge of all of the facts contained within all of the schedules and exhibits attached to this agreement.

8. *Debts*

The parties agree that neither shall use the credit of the other without the written consent or written credit application of the other. Further, each agrees that neither shall be obligated for the present or future incurred debts of the other and shall hold the other party harmless therefrom, and shall pay for all costs and fees incurred by the other in preventing or defending against the collection of such debt.

9. *Inheritance*

Neither party shall have any right to inherit any portion of any gift, devise or bequest made by any person for the benefit of either party to this contract.

10. *Living Expenses*

10(a) (First Alternative)

The parties agree that each shall pay one half of all living expenses, said living expenses specifically defined as:

- Mortgage payment or rent
- Utilities
- Home care and maintenance
- Food
- Shared entertainment
- Medical expenses

10(a) (Second Alternative)

The parties agree to share equally all living expenses including but not limited to personal expenses as well as maintenance of a home unit.

10(a) (Third Alternative)

The parties agree to share responsibility for the following expenses, which shall be called the living expenses, in proportion to their respective incomes, or as otherwise specifically agreed herein; (______ % ____________ and ______ % ____________):

- Mortgage payment or rent
- Utilities
- Home care and maintenance
- Food
- Shared entertainment
- Medical expenses not covered by job-provided insurance

10(b) All other expenses not specifically set forth above shall be called personal expenses and shall be borne individually and separately by each of the parties.

11. *Joint Accounts*

In order to facilitate the payment of living expenses the parties shall open and maintain a joint checking account which shall be used exclusively for the payment of living expenses as hereinabove set forth. Each shall make contributions to said living expense account in amounts as set forth in this paragraph. In the event there are excess funds in said account the parties shall diminish their contributions therein, it being the intent of the parties that this account is solely for necessary living expenses. ____________ shall contribute $____ per month and ____________ shall contribute $____ per month.

12. *Illness*

The parties recognize that, in the absence of income by one of the parties resulting from unemployment or extended illness, living expenses shall become the sole responsibility of the other party for a period of _____ days (optional, 60 or 90 days, etc.); and in such situation the other party will assume responsibility for living expenses as defined above and including insurance, transportation and related transportation costs.

13. *Support Claims*

The parties understand that in the event of a termination of this relationship neither shall be liable to the other for any spousal support, rehabilitation funds, or any other payments for living expenses of any nature whatsoever. Each of the parties may choose to otherwise agree but such agreement shall be in writing and attached to this agreement and dated. Such circumstances may occur in the case of lengthy periods of unemployment or serious or prolonged illnesses of one or the other of the parties as set forth in paragraph 12 above.

ARTICLE II
CHILD SUPPORT (OPTIONAL)

________ has two children as a result of a prior marriage, which children shall reside with the parties.

It is understood that ________ has no obligation for the support of said children and has no intention of assuming any responsibility for the financial support and care of said children. ________'s former spouse, if any, may not rely upon this agreement or any of its terms, to reduce or prevent appropriate child support payments. None of the funds deposited into the joint account are intended for the use and/or benefit of said children.

ALTERNATIVE: Sole financial benefit to said children from this cohabitation is to the extent of ____________'s contribution to the joint account which in part is used for food and household expenses of the cohabitation unit.

ARTICLE III
EVALUATION

1. ________ and ________ recognize the possibility of change in this relationship and intend that this document shall be a focus for periodic evaluations of their financial commitments. The parties agree that either one can initiate a review of any article of the contract at any time for amendment in order to reflect any actual changes in their financial situation.

2. The parties agree that, in any event, there shall be an annual review of the provisions of the contract, including any additions to jointly owned property. Changes are not mandatory and cannot be imposed upon either party.

3. Gifts by one party to another shall remain the sole property of the recipient, whatever the circumstances. A gift is defined as an item of personal property given over to the exclusive use of the recipient without written conditions.

ARTICLE IV
TERMINATION OF THE CONTRACT

1. Either party may, by individual desire or by mutual consent, terminate this contract and end the relationship at any time by written notification.

2. In the event of a termination of the contract and in the event that joint assets have been acquired, whether real or personal, and except for season tickets of any nature, said assets shall be listed and sold forthwith at market price. Each party shall take all steps necessary and shall execute all documents necessary to carry out the intent of this paragraph.

3. The parties may agree not to sell jointly held assets but said agreement shall be in writing and signed and dated by both parties before the asset may be retained.

4. Season tickets shall be used alternatively by each party, the first of such times to be determined by chance.

5. In the event one of the parties fails to carry out any of the terms contained in this article or in any article of this agreement or in any recital contained herein, the party desiring to enforce this agreement shall petition, make an appropriate motion or apply to any civil court of competent jurisdiction to appoint one independent arbitrator. The arbitrator shall arbitrate the dispute and shall be empowered to issue a judgment enforceable in the state in which the arbitration was held. Arbitration costs and fees shall be borne by the party losing the dispute or as determined by the arbitrator. All necessary or initial costs of commencement shall be borne by the party requiring the arbitration who shall be reimbursed in accordance with the judgment rendered.

6. The state of ________ shall be the state of jurisdiction over this contract.

7. In the event of the termination of the contract the provisions contained herein shall serve as the final Property Settlement Agreement of the parties, including but not limited to property rights, support rights, inheritance, and homestead rights. Marriage of the parties shall not terminate this agreement.

8. (Optional) In the event a child is born of this relationship nothing herein is intended to nor shall it affect the rights of the child or the obligations of either party to support and care for said child.

9. Each of the parties has read this agreement and each paragraph of it individually and together. None of the terms may be changed by oral agreement or conduct to the contrary notwithstanding any law or statutes in any state or territory of the United States.

________________________ ________________________

Date

____

Each party has stated that he or she understands and agrees with the terms of this contract.

Witness:

________________________ ________________________

Date

Duplicate

Cohabitation Agreement
of
____________ and ____________

THIS CONTRACT is entered into the ______ day of ________ ____________, 19__, by and between ____________ and ____________.

RECITALS

1. The undersigned parties (live together) or (intend to live together) but do not intend to marry and do not intend to have their legal relationship governed by the provisions of any state or federal domestic relations or family law statute or ruling. They shall be bound by this agreement and general contract principles.

2. The parties have together assisted one another in defining the terms of this cohabitation agreement and seek by this agreement to preserve and promote their individual privacy and identities.

3. The contract is not intended to nor does it encourage or discourage the relationship. The parties have entered into this contract solely to specify their agreement with regard to the ownership of real and personal property and to specify their relationship to all financial matters which may arise during and after the time they live together.

4. Each party has read this contract and understands all of the terms of the contract and understands that the agreements contained herein are binding in all respects. Each freely and in good faith chooses to enter into this cohabitation contract and fully intends it to be binding in every respect.

5. (*Use where applicable*) The party or parties, ______ and/or ______, have sought the advice of (friends) (an attorney) (relatives) before executing this agreement and have had the opportunity therefore to reflect upon all of the terms contained herein and agree that the terms are fair and reasonable.

ARTICLE I
PROPERTY, DEBTS AND LIVING EXPENSES

____________ and ____________ intend that the individual autonomy sought in the relationship shall be reflected in ownership of existing and future acquired property, in the characterization and control of income, and in the responsibility of each for living expenses and acquisition of necessary items of personal property which enable the relationship to appropriately exist. None of the terms herein depend upon the nature of the relationship between us.

1. *Property*

(a) The parties have made full disclosure to each other of all properties and assets presently owned by each of them and have described the income derived therefrom and from all other sources and agree that each party shall have sole management, control, and disposition of the property or assets specifically described in Schedule A, which is the separate property of ________, and Schedule B, which is the separate property of ________, both of which schedules are attached hereto, incorporated by reference and made a part of this contract. All earnings of each from any source whatsoever or earnings based on the existing separate property assets of each belong to each until and unless commingled or otherwise specified in this agreement.

1(a) (First Alternative)

There is no real or personal property at the present time which is owned jointly by the parties with the exception of those items listed as jointly owned items on Schedules A and B. Neither party desires to reveal to the other a specific list of all properties or assets owned other than as set forth in the schedules and is willing to accept the risk of possible later confusion resulting from this refusal.

1(a) (Second Alternative)

There is no real or personal property at the present time which is owned jointly by the parties except as set forth in Schedule A attached hereto and incorporated herein. Neither party desires to reveal to the other a specific list of assets or all properties and assets owned. However, each has prepared a separate list of properties and assets and has sealed the list in an envelope marked with their name thereon, which envelope is attached hereto and which shall remain sealed until and unless the parties or either one of them desire to terminate the relationship. The envelope shall be dated the day of the execution of this agreement and each schedule contained therein shall be fully dated.

2. *Earnings*

The parties agree that the wages, salary, other income, whether earnings or otherwise, or other distributions derived or received by either of the parties will be the separate property of such party and subject to the independent control and/or obligation of such party. In order to avoid the commingling of separate assets the parties shall maintain separate bank accounts, except as otherwise specified herein.

3. *Acquisitions*

All property, whether real or personal, acquired hereafter by either party during this relationship, whether by gift, inheritance, or any other means whatsoever, or derived as income generated from such property, shall belong exclusively to the party acquiring it and the other party shall acquire no rights in such asset.

4. *Joint Acquisitions*

In the event the parties acquire jointly any property, real, personal or otherwise, the ownership of said property will be determined in accordance with the respective monetary contributions of each party. No other method of pro rata ownership evaluation shall be employed.

5. *Joint Acquisitions—Alternative*

The parties may, by written agreement only, determine their respective interests in any item of property on a basis other than financial contribution, but such agreement shall not be effective unless written and signed. There shall be no oral transmutation of property from one status to another. We cannot, by conduct or oral statements, change the ownership of our respective property.

6. (Optional)

Annually, or sooner if necessary, the parties agree to amend Schedules A and B of this contract to include future acquired separate or joint property and any changes in the ownership of property presently described in said Schedules A and B.

7. *Voluntary Act*

Each party acknowledges that he or she has read all of the exhibits mentioned above and that each is entering into this agreement freely, voluntarily, and with full knowledge of all of the facts contained within all of the schedules and exhibits attached to this agreement.

8. *Debts*

The parties agree that neither shall use the credit of the other without the written consent or written credit application of the other. Further, each agrees that neither shall be obligated for the present or future incurred debts of the other and shall hold the other party harmless therefrom, and shall pay for all costs and fees incurred by the other in preventing or defending against the collection of such debt.

9. *Inheritance*

Neither party shall have any right to inherit any portion of any gift, devise or bequest made by any person for the benefit of either party to this contract.

10. *Living Expenses*

10(a) (First Alternative)

The parties agree that each shall pay one half of all living expenses, said living expenses specifically defined as:

- Mortgage payment or rent
- Utilities
- Home care and maintenance
- Food
- Shared entertainment
- Medical expenses

10(a) (Second Alternative)

The parties agree to share equally all living expenses including but not limited to personal expenses as well as maintenance of a home unit.

10(a) (Third Alternative)

The parties agree to share responsibility for the following expenses, which shall be called the living expenses, in proportion to their respective incomes, or as otherwise specifically agreed herein; (______ % ____________ and ______ % ____________):

- Mortgage payment or rent
- Utilities
- Home care and maintenance
- Food
- Shared entertainment
- Medical expenses not covered by job-provided insurance

10(b) All other expenses not specifically set forth above shall be called personal expenses and shall be borne individually and separately by each of the parties.

11. *Joint Accounts*

In order to facilitate the payment of living expenses the parties shall open and maintain a joint checking account which shall be used exclusively for the payment of living expenses as hereinabove set forth. Each shall make contributions to said living expense account in amounts as set forth in this paragraph. In the event there are excess funds in said account the parties shall diminish their contributions therein, it being the intent of the parties that this account is solely for necessary living expenses. ____________ shall contribute $____ per month and ______________ shall contribute $____ per month.

12. *Illness*

The parties recognize that, in the absence of income by one of the parties resulting from unemployment or extended illness, living expenses shall become the sole responsibility of the other party for a period of ______ days (optional, 60 or 90 days, etc.); and in such situation the other party will assume responsibility for living expenses as defined above and including insurance, transportation and related transportation costs.

13. *Support Claims*

The parties understand that in the event of a termination of this relationship neither shall be liable to the other for any spousal support, rehabilitation funds, or any other payments for living expenses of any nature whatsoever. Each of the parties may choose to otherwise agree but such agreement shall be in writing and attached to this agreement and dated. Such circumstances may occur in the case of lengthy periods of unemployment or serious or prolonged illnesses of one or the other of the parties as set forth in paragraph 12 above.

ARTICLE II
CHILD SUPPORT (OPTIONAL)

_________ has two children as a result of a prior marriage, which children shall reside with the parties.

It is understood that _________ has no obligation for the support of said children and has no intention of assuming any responsibility for the financial support and care of said children. _________'s former spouse, if any, may not rely upon this agreement or any of its terms, to reduce or prevent appropriate child support payments. None of the funds deposited into the joint account are intended for the use and/or benefit of said children.

ALTERNATIVE: Sole financial benefit to said children from this cohabitation is to the extent of _____________'s contribution to the joint account which in part is used for food and household expenses of the cohabitation unit.

ARTICLE III
EVALUATION

1. ________ and ________ recognize the possibility of change in this relationship and intend that this document shall be a focus for periodic evaluations of their financial commitments. The parties agree that either one can initiate a review of any article of the contract at any time for amendment in order to reflect any actual changes in their financial situation.

2. The parties agree that, in any event, there shall be an annual review of the provisions of the contract, including any additions to jointly owned property. Changes are not mandatory and cannot be imposed upon either party.

3. Gifts by one party to another shall remain the sole property of the recipient, whatever the circumstances. A gift is defined as an item of personal property given over to the exclusive use of the recipient without written conditions.

ARTICLE IV
TERMINATION OF THE CONTRACT

1. Either party may, by individual desire or by mutual consent, terminate this contract and end the relationship at any time by written notification.

2. In the event of a termination of the contract and in the event that joint assets have been acquired, whether real or personal, and except for season tickets of any nature, said assets shall be listed and sold forthwith at market price. Each party shall take all steps necessary and shall execute all documents necessary to carry out the intent of this paragraph.

3. The parties may agree not to sell jointly held assets but said agreement shall be in writing and signed and dated by both parties before the asset may be retained.

4. Season tickets shall be used alternatively by each party, the first of such times to be determined by chance.

5. In the event one of the parties fails to carry out any of the terms contained in this article or in any article of this agreement or in any recital contained herein, the party desiring to enforce this agreement shall petition, make an appropriate motion or apply to any civil court of competent jurisdiction to appoint one independent arbitrator. The arbitrator shall arbitrate the dispute and shall be empowered to issue a judgment enforceable in the state in which the arbitration was held. Arbitration costs and fees shall be borne by the party losing the dispute or as determined by the arbitrator. All necessary or initial costs of commencement shall be borne by the party requiring the arbitration who shall be reimbursed in accordance with the judgment rendered.

6. The state of ________ shall be the state of jurisdiction over this contract.

7. In the event of the termination of the contract the provisions contained herein shall serve as the final Property Settlement Agreement of the parties, including but not limited to property rights, support rights, inheritance, and homestead rights. Marriage of the parties shall not terminate this agreement.

8. (Optional) In the event a child is born of this relationship nothing herein is intended to nor shall it affect the rights of the child or the obligations of either party to support and care for said child.

9. Each of the parties has read this agreement and each paragraph of it individually and together. None of the terms may be changed by oral agreement or conduct to the contrary notwithstanding any law or statutes in any state or territory of the United States.

____________________ ____________________

Date

____

Each party has stated that he or she understands and agrees with the terms of this contract.

Witness:

____________________ ____________________

Date

V. Questions and Answers

1. Do these contracts hold up? What have the courts held?

Answer: The agreement relies on well-recognized contractual principles throughout the fifty states. It is, in fact, no different from any other contract even though it arises from a modern relationship. Courts have called similar agreements "highly favored" and "to be encouraged." The reason is that courts will avoid deciding such matters if they can reasonably be avoided.

The agreement is enforceable in all states as set forth in its terms. It contains no language to make it contrary to recognized public policy. It is not essentially different from a partnership or joint venture contract.

2. Do you need a lawyer in order to have a valid cohabitation agreement?

Answer: No, you do not need a lawyer in order to have a valid agreement. The agreement contained in this book has been extracted from various appellate court cases. However, it is always advisable to see an attorney. An attorney can be a witness to the fact that each party understands what they are doing and that details of the agreement have been carefully read and considered. More detailed analyses and variations can be explained.

3. Can this agreement be enforced in all states?

Answer: Absolutes do not exist in the law but the agreement is based upon contract law and principles. It is not based upon special laws of marriage or cohabitation in any state and it is not based upon the nature of the relationship of the parties, whether they are mere roommates or otherwise.

4. What are the advantages of cohabitating?

Answer: There are several important advantages, including the retaining of social security benefits after the age of sixty-two. Each person over the age of sixty-two is entitled to certain social security benefits which may be lost in part or in whole by marrying. Before the mature person considers remarriage, inquiry should be made with the social security administration as to what rights are retained and what rights are lost. After that you should consult with all the family relatives and with one another, and with your attorney.

Pension rights can be lost by marriage. Medical and disability rights under various pension plans can be lost by marriage. But you probably cannot be covered under one another's medical insurance policies when you cohabit. Medicare rights cannot be transferred or assigned and cannot cover the person you live with.

Another advantage is simplicity. Cohabiting is less likely to cause confusing circumstances than a marriage. Marriage causes some very clear rights to accrue to each of the parties barring some special contract. A premarital contract may do. However, a contract between parties who are cohabiting is easier to deal with.

5. Can you be cohabiting if you live with someone part-time, such as on weekends?

Answer: It is highly improbable that a weekend arrangement can be defined so as to give rise to any property rights in either of the parties.

6. Can you change the agreement?

Answer: Yes. But you can change it only by an entirely new written agreement, a deletion or modification of part of the old, or an addition or ADDENDUM to be added to the end. Changes on the original agreement should be signed and dated. The ADDENDUM must be signed and dated. It is a good idea to have the change witnessed and the parties state they understand the modification. Read it to the witness to see if he or she also understands.

There is an exception to the above rule. You can change the agreement orally so long as the *oral* change is carried out and *completed* in every respect. Other than this exception the contract prevents oral changes.

7. Suppose we do acquire things jointly from jointly contributed funds, what happens if we split up?

Answer: If you can't agree quickly on any other disposition, sell the item. Don't let it become a hassle. The contract covers this. When you agree on a dispostion write it down and sign and date it.

8. Is it necessary to list everything that each of you claims ownership in as separate property?

Answer: Absolutely. A failure to include any single piece of property, especially a business, whether an unincorporated association, partnership or otherwise, could be a serious and fatal mistake. Leaving out the asset may be the same as an interpretation that there was an intent that *both* parties own one half each of that asset. It is not necessary to list spoons and forks and things of that nature. You may generally categorize such small items. However, it is advisable to list everything in a relatively high degree of detail and to describe the items in such a way that they can be identified without question. For instance, do not define dishes as "dishes"; describe such items as "white china dishes with gold ring," etc.

9. What if you are cohabiting with one person and having an affair with another?

Answer: If you are cohabiting with *anyone* marital types of rights can and sometimes do arise. They do not arise with people who are simply having an affair, and are not permanently cohabiting.

10. Should either party put property into both of their names as joint tenants or property as tenants in common without an agreement?

Answer: No. Not unless you want a court to arrange the end of the *partnership*. Putting property in the name of both of the parties binds them to that situation totally without a specifically agreed-upon way *out* when their relationship ends.

11. What happens if you have a successful cohabitation?

Answer: You will probably get married. If you are over sixty you must inquire how this would affect your expected social security rights. If each of you earns an above-average income, talk to an accountant about how this would affect your tax situation. The agreement in this book might have to be changed or modified. The mere fact of marriage does not change or terminate the contract. It makes this point clear. However, either of you may, at any time, terminate the agreement as provided.

12. Do persons who cohabit have rights to inherit from the estate of the other?

Answer: Nobody knows. Strict logic would seem to dictate that rights of inheritance would arise in the same manner that marital rights would arise. But the courts would be loath to extend these principles so far into the laws of inheritance and into family life. Too much general upset with other claimants would occur, such as sisters, brothers, sons and daughters, and the like. My guess is that the courts would find a way out of the situation by simply calling it against public policy to have such rights accrue.

The problem of quarrels over an inheritance arises because of conflicting claims as to what property belongs to the estate of the deceased and what property belongs to the cohabitee.

13. Can you create joint property without cohabiting?

Answer: Yes. This is no different from two people getting together and buying property jointly in various pro-rata shares.

14. Suppose you cohabit with one person but are still legally married to another? What happens to the property rights of either of the parties?

Answer: The rights to earnings or interests in the earnings or the earning capacity of married people *after* they are separated generally no longer exist. In other words, when married people physically separate or make a determination that they are not going to live together any longer the rights of each to the other's earnings or the accumulations of his or her work efforts cease. However, all existing assets acquired up until that time remain the joint or community assets of the parties. This rule varies from state to state so you must consult a local attorney.

15. What do we do to make the agreement valid?

Answer: The agreement does not need to be filed or lodged or placed in any special location or with any special party. It is very important to have the agreement signed in front of a witness who can testify not only that the signatures are genuine, but that the persons who are signing the agreement are in fact the persons they represent themselves to be. Any person can do this and any notary in any state can also do this for you. You should sign at least two agreements and mark a third as a copy. Each party should have one fully completed and signed and notarized agreement. The third agreement should be marked "copy" with all of the signatures and the notary's seal printed on it with the appropriate dates and locations. It should be initialed on the signature page by the parties and placed in a neutral safe-deposit box or with someone's relative or lawyer. The duplicate originals should be kept by each of the parties, preferably in a safe-deposit box where access can be had instantly by an interested family member other than one another. A notarial acknowledgment is preferred, not required.

Many savings and loan associations will provide free safe-deposit boxes for each account opened and this provides a simple means for each party to keep their own agreement safe and intact.

16. Can you mistakenly cause liabilities to arise in a cohabiting situation?

Answer: Yes. Often loan applications, charge account applications and similar credit arrangements are made by *both* of the parties. When the two parties split up they both remain liable even though it may have been only one of the parties who did most of the charging. Maintaining separate credit or joint credit with the knowledge of what the problems may become is wise. You should consult your local attorney about the particular creditor-debtor relation laws of that state. However, without exception, joint application for credit means that both persons will be jointly and separately liable for the *entire* amount.

17. Do you need a notary to sign it to acknowledge your signature?

Answer: No, but it's a very good idea. The notary should be treated as if he were a witness, as previously explained. Any notary can affix to the contract an appropriate notarial form from the state and county in which you reside.

18. What if you have children during the period of cohabitation?

Answer: The rights of children are never inhibited by the failure of the parties to be married. The only time that the rights of children are affected is when the male member of the cohabitation relationship denies that the child is his child. Then the customary laws of proving who is the father of the child for your particular jurisdiction will be involved. Usually this involves a lawsuit to establish paternity and these lawsuits are almost exactly the same in every state and require almost the same amount of proof. There are new blood tests that almost perfectly pinpoint who is or is not the father of a child. The ability of the modern male to deny the existence of paternity is almost nil.

Rights of inheritance of the children remain intact and the right to be supported by both parents remains intact irrespective of marriage. So long as both parties acknowledge the children as their own the children's rights are not affected.

19. Is there such a thing as common law marriage so that you become married without actually going through a ceremony?

Answer: In most states there is no such thing as a common law spouse except where the term is used to describe the kind of relationship which became famous in the Lee Marvin case.

In those states where it does exist, the mere passage of time may create a marriage. If this happens you are living by the rules of the state unless you have a contract clarifying your intentions. Read the first paragraph of the contract in this book.

20. What if one party dies? Can the agreement be enforced?

Answer: Yes. The representative of the deceased person's estate can act in that person's place for all purposes and is bound by the contract.

21. Can homosexuals who are cohabiting have the same rights arise as heterosexuals?

Answer: Probably. This has not yet been decided in any appellate court in the United States to the best of my knowledge. However, we see no difference in the logic to be applied to a homosexual situation from that applied to a heterosexual situation. Note paragraph 3 of the contract. The rights of the parties do not result from the nature of the relationship. Mere roommates need contractual protection. The problem is in enforcing the technical and legal rights which may arise.

22. How does arbitration work?

Answer: Arbitration is a substitute for civil court action. It is more informal and not subject to the strict rules of civil and court proceedings within any state judicial system. Disputes can be resolved in much less time, with much less legal and technical involvement of lawyers. Therefore it is cheaper. A court is empowered to appoint an arbitrator if the parties can't agree on one.

23. Should a lawyer review the contract before you sign it?

Answer: You may have questions not anticipated herein or special circumstances. Also, neither of you can try that old cliché, "I didn't know what I was signing." In the event you do not use a lawyer to explain things, your witness or your notary should be *told aloud* by each of you that you understand. Sounds like a useless gesture, but it isn't.

24. Is there anything technical to be reminded of?

Answer: Yes. Initial all crossouts and changes on the contract form. Initial each page of the contract as well as signing it. Two original duplicates, fully signed and initialed, and an extra copy marked "copy" will do. Do the same with all subsequent changes and date each one as explained.

25. Explain the Marvin case.

Answer: A California court held that parties can agree by conduct or otherwise that they are to share in the earnings and assets of both while they cohabit. Many states are dealing with this situation now. After ten years Michelle Triola and Lee Marvin split and the Marvin Rule developed. The famous trial was to determine the issue of whether a contract—oral, implied, written or by conduct—existed. The trial judge determined that it did not but that Michelle was entitled to "rehabilitation money" anyway.

This was changed on appeal. The law has gone no further in clarifying cohabitation rights in any other jurisdiction so far as is known at the date of this writing. However, expansion of cohabitation rights is going on all the time. In California a cohabitee was granted unemployment compensation when she moved with her loved one to another state and an unmarried woman collected death benefits after the man she was living with was killed in an industrial accident.

That is why the cohabitation contract in this book *does not* rely on any of these "marital" or vague "living together" principles, or upon conduct or oral promises.

26. Can cohabitation affect custody rights?

Answer: The interests and well-being of the children come first. The precise issue has not arisen in the courts of all states. In most states the mere fact of cohabitation would be irrelevant to the question of being a fit and proper parent.

One state decided otherwise but the decision is generally considered to be a return to the eighteenth century. Indeed, the law generally is that a court must consider the interests of the children first. Everything else is secondary. This is how you should be guided. The interest and well-being of the children come first.

27. Can cohabitation give rise to property rights even though you are still married to another?

Answer: Yes. While married to one person you can begin to live with another. People seem to need this emotional help while the marriage is in its last gasp. Given sufficient time—and no one can supply a precise measure of time—the roommate and the abandoned husband or wife can have conflicting claims. If jointly owned property with a spouse is improved while living with a roommate—cohabitee—each might claim an interest in a portion of the asset. Further, if roommate assists spouse in hiding assets from another spouse the conspirators would both be liable for the hidden services or assets. If your divorce is taking forever, do not start living with another person without the contract in this book.

28. The Future.

No one can predict how far and wide the rights of persons can extend in cohabiting situations. The law is developing constantly with all the nuances that exist in life itself. Accordingly, wisdom dictates that you attend to business as advised in this book.